CONTENTS

The Writing Prompts Workbook, Grades 7-8:
Story Starters for Journals, Assignments and More

Bryan Cohen

Edited by Debra Cohen and Amy Crater.

DEDICATION

I dedicate this book to all the bookworms and writers languishing in middle school just waiting for the time when they will be able to shine.

INTRODUCTION

Welcome to *The Writing Prompts Workbook*! Within these pages you'll find 200 writing prompts, two on each page, that will help to stimulate the imagination of your students or children. I've found that the key to allowing students to fully latch onto an idea is to give them a scenario followed by a question. In answering the question, young writers can take the same prompt a million different directions. You may even want to try photocopying a page and have your writers take on the same prompt at the beginning and the end of a school year just to see how different their storytelling has become.

The Writing Prompts Workbook series is a collection of books I've created after seeing how many parents and teachers have visited my website, Build Creative Writing Ideas (located at http://www.build-creative-writing-ideas.com). I have adapted my thousands of prompts into six workbooks designed to take a first grader creatively all the way up through the end of high school. The six books are available for grades 1-2, 3-4, 5-6, 7-8, 9-10 and 11-12. The prompts become more complex with each volume, but continue to remain imaginative and creative throughout.

I love hearing about the progress of students on my site and I'm always interested in hearing new ideas for delivering creative writing prompts to writers from the ages of five to 105. Feel free to contact me on my website for any questions and comments you can think of. I hope you and your future best-selling authors thoroughly enjoy this and future books in the series. Happy writing!

Sincerely,
Bryan Cohen
Author of *The Writing Prompts Workbook* Series

PS: While there is space below each prompt for your budding writers to write, there is a good chance they may have more to say than they can fit on the page. There is an extra page in the back if you'd like to photocopy it, but I strongly suggest that you also get a notebook and some extra pencils just in case. A dictionary for challenging words may also be helpful.

Name _____ Date _____

1. Imagine that you were a part of the first Thanksgiving between the American Indians and the Pilgrims. What would your role be in such a feast and what are some things you would notice that didn't make it into the history books?

2. Whether a result of marriage, being away at school or some other unforeseen circumstance, almost everybody has spent at least one Thanksgiving away from his or her family. What would your first turkey day without family be like and how would it be different from your traditional holiday meal?

Name _____ Date _____

3. If your Thanksgiving turkey could wake up and talk to you and
your family what would it say and why? Would you still eat him after he spoke his piece?

4. Create a story of a perfect Thanksgiving meal from beginning of the day until the last
dish is washed. Who is there, what food is available and what activities do you all
participate in to make the holiday the most memorable in existence?

Name _____ Date _____

5. You have the choice to invite five guests, dead or alive, to your Thanksgiving dinner to share in your food, family and friendly conversation. Who are they, why do you choose them and what is it like dining with them?

6. Even though some of the biggest parts of this holiday revolve around food, it's important to remember to give thanks. What are some of the things you are most grateful about from the last year? What are some things you hope to be thankful for in the coming year?

Name _____ Date _____

7. Imagine that you and your childhood friends were involved in a wild Thanksgiving Day adventure. What happens on this crazy day and are you able to keep the traditions of the holiday alive?

8. You have been chosen to design a new float for the Macy's Thanksgiving Day Parade. What do you decide to design and why? How do the announcers and the viewing public respond to your stunning creation?

Name _____ Date _____

9. In last ditch effort to fly home for Thanksgiving, your plane was stranded hundreds of miles away from home at an airport. To salvage the holiday, you and the other passengers from the stranded plane resolve to have a Thanksgiving meal at the airport itself. Describe the meal and the new people you meet during this alternative holiday gathering.

10. Imagine that you were in a room full of the important people who decided on the symbols of Thanksgiving. Sure, they ended up deciding on turkey, stuffing and cranberry sauce, but before those food staples, they came up with hundreds of rejected Thanksgiving ideas. What were some of the rejected ideas? Which were the best and which were the worst?

Name _____ Date _____

11. You have been given a time machine and can travel to any point in the history of the Earth. Where will you travel and why? What is your first week like in this new time period?

12. If you could fast forward ahead or rewind backwards to any point in your life, when would it be and why? Be very detailed about how you deal with this second chance or sneak peak.

Name _____ Date _____

13. As you get older there are lots of new things that you'll be
allowed to do. Within the next 15 to 20 years, you'll be able to drive, go to college and
maybe even get your own apartment. What are some of the things you look forward to
during that time?

14. Some say that the American Dream is to grow up, get married and have two kids living
in a nice house with a white picket fence. Is that your American Dream? Why or why not?
If not, describe what your dream future would be like.

Name _____ Date _____

15. Your mom has had a crazy week of taking care of the family and you decide to make her breakfast in bed. What do you cook her and how do you present it to her? What is her reaction to your kind gesture?

16. The famous inventor of the light bulb, Thomas Edison, created hundreds of other inventions with his team during his lifetime. If you could invent five new things that had never previously existed, what would they be? Go into detail, especially about what they do.

Name _____ Date _____

17. Imagine that you had to live an entire day in slow motion. How would things be different? Would you get bored having the whole day take double the time or longer?

18. If you and all of your friends had a big picnic, but each of you could only bring one item, what do you think you would all bring? List each of your friends and write a sentence or two about what each of them would add to the mix.

Name _____ Date _____

19. What do you think it is about a person that makes them have a
good or a bad sense of fashion? What are the things that a guy should wear and what are
the things that a girl should wear? How would you rate your own fashion sense on a scale
of 1 to 10 and why?

20. Gratitude is a feeling you have when you are happy to have something or someone in
your life. What are five things that you are grateful for and why? Why do you think some
people have a hard time being grateful?

Name _____ Date _____

21. You are standing on the edge of the sand right before your feet hit the water. You stare out into the ocean. Write a story about the many thoughts going through your head.

22. Write a story about a child building a sand castle and talking through the entire story of the medieval town he is creating. The king, the queen, the knights, and all the people inside are given personalities and histories. Be as detailed as possible.

Name _____ Date _____

23. Imagine that you are a crab walking along on the ocean. It's a complicated job trying to avoid all of the people while trying to get a bit of food from every passerby at the same time. Talk about a day in the life of Herbert J. Crab (or whatever your name is).

24. Talk about a sport that you've played on the beach, whether a simple game of catch or some kind of water football. Who did you play with and how did the game go? If you've never done this, make up a story about it.

Name _____ Date _____

25. What is the most beautiful beach that you've ever been to?
Describe the entire scene thoroughly and explain why the beach was such a pretty sight to behold. If you have never been to an aesthetically pleasing beach, create a story in which you had.

26. What would be your perfect beach day? Describe the weather and the people you would be going with? Who would you see there and what activities would be occurring during your perfect stay?

Name _____ Date _____

27. You have just gotten out from school for the year and it's time to
go to camp. What friends are you looking forward to seeing? What activities will you do?

28. It's the annual "Dad takes us camping" trip. Is this an event you look forward to or not?
If you never had such a trip, imagine it, and write about how it'd go.

Name _____ Date _____

29. It's the biggest camping danger cliché ever: A bear! What do you do to avoid getting mauled?

30. What is the best campfire ghost story you've ever heard? If you've never heard one, make one up!

Name _____ Date _____

31. It's the middle of the night and you are a counselor for a camp of
about 30 kids. The kids' tent collapses in the middle of the night. What happens and how
do you deal with it?

32. What is your favorite camping activity? Is it fishing, games, campfires, or nature?
Create a story in which you and your best friends are doing this favorite activity.

Name _____ Date _____

33. If you could camp anywhere in the world, where would it be and why? Go into extreme detail.

34. You are out camping with a grown up and he falls ill. You must lead the two of you back to safety. What do you do?

Name _____ Date _____

35. The crackling campfire can be so peaceful. Talk about sitting around one with your best friends.

36. You and your friends come upon an old cabin in the woods. What do you do?

Name _____ Date _____

37. Describe a situation in which you were the coldest you've ever been in your life during the winter.

38. It's probably difficult to remember your first snowfall as a child. Do a sort of bird's eye view account of what that experience could have been like for "little you."

Name _____ Date _____

39. After a big snowstorm, you and your family are trapped in the house with no place to go for at least the next 48 hours. What do you do with this time?

40. Ice skating on natural ice! Talk about a time in which you skated on real ice (not in a rink). Make up the story if you don't have one.

Name _____ Date _____

41. It is - 10 degrees F outside. What do you wear? Detail your dressing process for the extreme cold.

42. You are building the most extreme snow display ever. Not just a snowman but an entire snow city! Talk about you and your fellow builders creating such beauty.

Name _____ Date _____

43. You and your school face off against another school in an epic snowball extravaganza. Detail the entire battle.

44. Driving on snow and ice takes a great deal of patience and skill. Create a story about a long winter driving trip.

Name _____ Date _____

45. Sitting by a roaring fireplace, sipping a hot cocoa, while bundled
up in a fleece blanket. Talk about how wonderful this can be in the dead of winter.

46. What is your favorite past experience that occurred during the season of winter. Be
very specific.

Name _____ Date _____

47. It's the first warm, pleasant day of the spring season. What kind of activities do you do outside to embrace the day?

48. It's April and you know what the means: April Showers. Big time! Talk about living through a month of nearly all spring-time rain.

Name _____ Date _____

49. Spring cleaning! Create a story in which you have to sort through a lot of prized memorabilia from your past. What do you keep and what do you throw away?

50. You are in a meadow that truly shows the beauty of spring. There is green everywhere punctuated by other bright colors. You close your eyes and breathe in. What is going through your mind?

Name _____ Date _____

51. You go out of your front door and you're confronted by...bees! A
spring hive of bees has formed near your front door. Write the story about you dealing with
the hive. Remember that bees are an important part of the environment so just killing them
is not an option.

52. Time for some spring fruit picking with your family! Describe a time where your
family fruit picked. This story can be made up or exaggerated if you wish.

Name _____ Date _____

53. Talk about your experiences with spring sports. This could be connected to Spring Training, field hockey, lacrosse (really anything spring season and sport-related).

54. Imagine that you have a $100 bill in your wallet. You go to the grocery store and after making purchases you spend exactly $100. When you look back in your wallet you see that there is another $100. You spend it again. It comes back! Detail your first week with this ever replenishing $100 bill.

Name _____ Date _____

55. You have just won a great sum of money from the lottery to be divvied out in $1,000 increments each week for the rest of your life. What will you do with this newly added income? Describe your first year with this exciting addition to your life.

56. After a freak accident (resembling a comic book origin story) you gain the ability to receive everything that you think about. How do you use this newfound power to increase your money, your possessions, and your charity?

Name _____ Date _____

57. Your hard work on a screenplay has paid off! Not only have you sold your first one for $500,000, but a powerful Hollywood executive has asked you to complete a 5 picture deal, making double that amount on each progressive script. Talk about the changes in your life that have occurred from this new offer. How does this change your family, friends, and living arrangements?

58. A wealthy relative has passed away, leaving you her entire estate. She asks that you use this money to secure your future and to improve the conditions of the community she grew up in. Talk about the step by step plan you create and how people around you react to your decisions.

Name _____ Date _____

59. A few strokes of luck have propelled you through the social
ranks. You now call several big celebrities your friends and they have given you enough
opportunities to make almost ten times the money you make now. How do you balance this
new social lifestyle with your work and home life?

60. You have $100,000 to give to whatever charities you want. Pick, choose, and visit each
of these charities directly, getting a chance to see exactly where your money has gone.

Name _____ Date _____

61. Write a story about a time that you were injured, whether it was a small injury or a more serious one. How did you deal with the problem and what kind of medical attention did you receive? If it was a long time ago and you don't quite remember, fill in some made-up details.

62. What is the most sick you have ever been? What caused it and what did you have to do to recover your health? Go into the deep and gross detail, as you may get some effective new ways to describe things from such an exercise.

Name _____ Date _____

63. Write about your favorite and least favorite doctors throughout
your lifetime. What made them so memorable? Who treated you the best? Who treated you
the worst? Create a conversation between the three of you all at the same time, where you
try to get the bad doctors to understand a better way of doing things.

64. Detail a story that draws from an experience in which you had to care for someone who
was ill or injured. How did you help him or her to feel better and what did you learn in the
process?

Name _____ Date _____

65. Have you ever feared for your life during an injury or illness?
Talk about those feelings and if you haven't, create a story in which you felt in danger for your life. What happened and how did you make a complete recovery?

66. Describe the most memorable meal you've ever had in your whole life (good or bad).
Go into detail of the people who were there with you (if any), the courses that were served, the location of the meal, and how you felt before and after.

Name _____ Date _____

67. Depending on what type of meal (good or bad) you chose in
prompt #1, go the opposite direction, and describe a meal that had the opposite effect on
you. Go into the same detail of the people, courses, location, and feelings that you had.

68. Detail a fantastical evening in which you create the perfect meal, the perfect ambiance,
and invite the perfect people. Elaborate greatly on the preparation and the reactions of your
esteemed guests.

Name _____ Date _____

69. Write about eating an entire bowl of fruit. Feel free to make the fruits as exotic and interesting as possible. Really play on the use of all five senses with this exercise.

70. Your good friend has invited you over for...pretty much the worst smelling and tasting meal you've ever experienced. Describe the entire encounter including every stomach churning bite.

Name _____ Date _____

71. You have been "volunteered" to cook for 100 people! Describe your day from the trip to the supermarket all the way through to the interminable clean up.

72. Though the book *Cloudy with a Chance of Meatballs* is fiction...giant portions of food begin raining down from the sky! How do you spend your first week in this new world where hunger is a memory and umbrellas are a necessity?

Name _____ Date _____

73. There's always that dish that "momma" made better than anybody else. It's something that you can't help but associate with home. Talk about the meal (or meals) that she created and what the memory of those meals means to you.

74. Create a science fiction or fantasy story using the scary sounding ingredients from a package of candy or ice cream!

Name _____ Date _____

75. Describe you and your friends/family as foods. Go into at least
five different people and describe what kinds of food they represent and why.

76. What is your favorite (or a few of your favorites) book and why? How many times
have you read it and how does it make you feel when you flip through the pages? What
would you tell someone when you're recommending this book to them?

Name _____ Date _____

77. What is your least favorite book? Why are you so turned off by it and how would you rail against it if a friend told you he was reading it? Now imagine that you are forced to watch a movie version of the book. Describe your experience.

78. Do you remember the first book that either you read or your parents read to you? Write a story comparing the reading of this first book to you versus you reading it to your child as his or her first book.

Name _____ Date _____

79. A friend has recommended that you read a book that he says is "completely amazing." The book is anything but. What do you tell your friend and does this change your opinion about his taste?

80. Talk about the book that you had the hardest time getting through in school (anything written by Faulkner for me!). Why do you think you had such a hard time and how did you do on any subsequent tests? How did you learn enough to get through the experience with a passing grade?

Name _____ Date _____

81. You have been transported into one of your favorite books as a character of your choosing. Who are you, what book is it, and what happens during your adventures? Go into extreme detail.

82. Sometimes, a friend, a parent, or a loved one just needs to take a few pieces of advice and their lives will begin to fall into place, you just know it. Take 5 people you know who need to stop being stubborn about certain things and pair each of them up with a different book. If they read this book they could benefit from the reading. What happens to them?

Name _____ Date _____

83. You have been given the chance to adapt a book of your choosing to the big screen! How do you go about making this book fit the typical 2 hour run time without losing any of your beloved or important elements?

84. What is your favorite place to read? Talk about why it is such a perfect spot and give a detailed account of one of your reading sessions including the book that you'd be most likely to read.

Name _____ Date _____

85. You are in a book club meeting! Talk about the various people
that would be in a book club of yours and what book you might be reading. Even if this has
never happened, make up your dream book club or the book club from hell.

86. You are writing the book of your dreams. How does it make you feel and what do you
think has held you back for so long from getting it completed?

Name _____ Date _____

87. You are walking down the road and you come upon a group of kids burning books. What do you do next?

88. A mob has taken down your girlfriend/boyfriend and imprisoned your family. Now it's time to get even! Discuss your infiltration of the mob's secret fortress and how you end up victorious against all odds?

Name _____ Date _____

89. Talk about a time in your life in which you were in a sort of action and adventure story. Did you have to show incredible athletic prowess or wits? Were there any big explosions? Go into extreme detail.

90. You are on the run from the police after being wrongfully accused for murder. Your only way of avoiding life in prison is to clear your name by finding the person who did this. What happens, how do you go about it, and how do you avoid capture?

Name _____ Date _____

91. You are a police officer involved in a high speed car chase. Go into extreme detail including all of the cars that get into accidents during your chase and how you attempt to catch the bad guys. Are you successful?

92. The bad guy almost always loses. Put yourself in the role of a criminal profiler who has to catch the bad guy during a big adventurous heist. The bad guy seems to have gotten away but from all your movie watching you know that there is still one last chance to catch him. How do you make sure that the bad guy slips up?

Name _____ Date _____

93. After a big explosion, you need to help rescue multiple people out of a burning building. Describe the experience from explosion onward. Are you successful?

94. In one of the biggest movie action scenes of all time, James Cameron gave us a feel of what it might have been like on the Titanic after its iceberg crash. Imagine that you are one of the passengers and you must avoid the many trials and tribulations of a sinking ship.

Name _____ Date _____

95. Imagine that you are the title character in any of the James Bond films. Imagine your experiences of avoiding and causing explosions, getting in one on one battles, and wining and dining beautiful vixens. A day in the life or a week in the life of this hero may give you enough material for a long while.

96. In a strange turn of events, you have found out that both of your parents are secret spies and that you have been thrown right into the middle of it. What does the reveal explain and how are you able to get out of a sticky situation that your parents have gotten into?

Name _____ Date _____

97. You are a hot-shot fighter pilot looking to take down an enemy battalion. How do you and your team go about it and do you emerge victorious? Go into extreme detail and look up plane information if you need to.

98. You have been hired to re-write an awful action flick. What is the movie and what do you change to make it not end up in the bargain bin within a few short years.

Name _____ Date _____

99. Today is a day like any other…except it was directed by Michael Bay (director of Transformers)! This famous Hollywood director is infamous for throwing as many explosions into a movie as possible. Write your day in the life directed by this special effects fanatic.

100. Describe the best piece of writing that you've ever written. What makes this the best in your mind? Also, write about what you think you would need to do to top it.

Name _____ Date _____

101. Describe the worst piece of writing that you've ever written. What did you learn from writing this piece?

102. Write a scene or story that is intentionally bad in every possible way.

Name _____ Date _____

103. Talk about a time in which someone praised your writing and how it made you feel. Describe the scene and the reactions of anybody else in the room upon hearing these words.

104. You have just won an award for your writing and you must give an acceptance speech that is worthy of your talents. Write your speech in its entirety and include an on-camera interview afterward for good measure.

Name _____ Date _____

105. Write a poem or a short story for the love of your life, past or present, real or imagined.

106. You have been given a magical pad of paper that makes everything that is written on it become reality. What do you write and what is your reasoning behind it?

Name _____ Date _____

107. Imagine a world in which writing was prized above athletics as
a worldwide televised sport and you are one of the top competitors. Describe this world
and what your "writing workout" would be.

108. How does writing fit into your life? Is it a hobby, a profession, a dream or something
else? Write about this priority and if you would like to shift it at some point.

Name _____ Date _____

109. Write the table of contents for your memoirs that you will be writing at the age of 80.

110. Talk about a time when a piece of writing changed you. Whether it is something you wrote or something you read, these words spoke to you and made you a different person. Describe how and why this piece made your world a different place.

Name _____ Date _____

111. You were digging around through some old stuff and you found some of your writing from the past. You cannot even remember writing it but it is truly amazing. Talk about what you do with it, who you show it to and what eventually happens as a result.

112. Re-write a scene from an awful book or movie. Make it better or play up the things that made it awful.

Name _____ Date _____

113. Talk about a time when your emotions affected your writing.
Did they affect them positively, negatively, subtly or some other way?

114. How do other people affect your writing? Talk about how a different people in your life change your writing after you interact with them.

Name _____ Date _____

115. Write a scene that portrays your ideal writing conditions.

116. Write a scene that portrays the conditions that make you not want to write a word.

Name _____ Date _____

117. Write a paragraph or two that you would write to somebody who is down on their luck. Make it an inspirational piece.

118. What is your favorite cartoon you remember from your childhood? What themes resonated with you as a child and how does it hold up today?

Name _____ Date _____

119. You have found yourself in the cartoon world of a popular movie or television show. How do you interact with the other characters and how does the style of animation affect you?

120. Which of the Disney princes or princesses would you be interested in starting a relationship with if they suddenly manifested into reality? What would a first date be like with that character?

Name _____ Date _____

121. How do you feel about the insurgence of computer-generated graphics in the world taking over for the typically hand-drawn work? Do you feel as though something has been lost as technology has improved?

122. In a cartoon battle, characters can pull out all of the stops, drawing weapons from nowhere and always surviving. Detail a cartoon battle between a hero and a villain to demonstrate how crazy it can get.

Name _____ Date _____

123. Pixar has set an extremely high bar when it comes to animated quality, but does it reach the quality of classic Disney cartoons? How do they compare and which one comes out on top?

124. If you could live out the adventures of one classic cartoon character who would it be and why?

Name _____ Date _____

125. How would your own life differ if it were made into a cartoon?
Would you be the main character? How would you take advantage of the new rules this world brings?

126. Pick a family cartoon like The Simpsons and write a scene in the same style with either people from your life or characters from the show.

Name _____ Date _____

127. You are given the opportunity to voice a cartoon character.
Describe your visit to the voice studio and how your character turns out when he makes it onto the screen.

128. If you could turn any of your writings into a cartoon movie or televisions show which would you choose and why? Describe the adaptation process with a creative team of producers and directors.

Name _____ Date _____

129. What is the most beautiful piece of music you've ever listened to? Talk about how each part of the song made you feel and why it has stuck with you. Also, relate a story in which you share it with someone else and try to convince them of its merit.

130. Write a story about a character (or draw from personal experience) in which that character creates some amazing music. This can be with any instrument (including a vocal one). What kind of song is it and how does the character feel about making it?

Name _____ Date _____

131. Describe your most enjoyable concert experience of all time.
What was the band, who did you go with, and why has it stuck with you as being so fantastic? Go into extreme detail and feel free to make use of any lyrics.

132. Most people have a genre of music that just does not appeal to them. What is yours and why? Create a dialogue between two characters: one who loves that genre and one (like you) who hates it.

Name _____ Date _____

133. You are the lead singer in a brand-new chart topping band!

How does it feel to be so famous for creating art? What is it like having so many fans and having to keep the band happy when egos begin to clash?

134. If you could be proficient in any one instrument what would it be and why? What would you do if you had immense talent in creating music with this instrument?

Name _____ Date _____

135. Have you ever had a piece of music change your life? What specifically changed you and why? If you haven't, just create a character or a piece of music that would cause such a thing to occur.

136. The television show "American Idol" has had thousands of people try out for a spot on the show. Create a story in which you go to audition (after practicing heavily I'm sure) and detail your experience at the tryout.

Name _____ Date _____

137. You have assembled an all-star team of producers and recording
artists to record the best music album ever. Who do you bring together and how does it go?

138. What would your life be without music and why?

Name _____ Date _____

139. You are out on the town the night that your city's team has won the World Series! You have been swept up in the crazy mob of fans and you will probably not be getting home until at least five in the morning. Describe your wild night.

140. Try to remember back to your first baseball game. The first time you saw semi-pro or professional players running about over the course of a wide expanse of grass or Astroturf. The first time you heard thousands of fans booing or cheering in unison for this game of bat and ball. Go into detail and if you can't remember something, make it up.

Name _____ Date _____

141. Describe a time in which you played some derivative of baseball. Whether it be the old ball and glove catch with your dad or friends or an actual full-length game. How did it go and how did it make you feel?

142. Put yourself in the shoes of a multi-million dollar superstar baseball player. Describe a typical baseball game day for you, keeping in mind your large expenses, your need to get to the field on time, the positive or negative fan response, and your trip back home.

Name _____ Date _____

143. Your town is all about high school baseball: they live it, breathe it, and revel in its success. You are a high school student and your best friend happens to be the star of the team. How does this friend react to this compartmentalized superstardom? Does he change from the person you knew or does he really leave it on the field?

144. If you could be transported to any period in baseball history for a few weeks, which one would it be? Babe Ruth's Yankees? Steve Carlton's Phillies? The Cubs 1908 world championship team? Talk about your experiences in this new time and place in which baseball history is taking place.

Name _____ Date _____

145. What was your best experience with baseball? Why was it so positive and how has it affected your life?

146. What was your worst experience with baseball? Why was it so negative and in what ways did it alter your outlook of the sport?

Name _____ Date _____

147. Describe yourself as a little boy or girl trying to catch a home run ball while surrounded by a bunch of drunken bleacher bums. Start at the at bat and go into minute detail as the ball comes your way.

148. Talk about (or make up) a time in which you went to a professional baseball game with a bunch of friends. Did you watch any of the game at all or did you just have fun being with your friends? Go into a lot of detail and have fun writing it.

Name _____ Date _____

149. You have become the owner of your favorite baseball team. How do you shake things up to keep your team winning?

150. Write a scene in which you explain baseball to someone who does not understand it at all.

Name _____ Date _____

151. Your boat has capsized about 20 miles off the coast of the ocean. Luckily, you have enough leg strength to keep yourself treading for a very long time. Describe the boat accident and your journey to safety over the next couple of days.

152. Try to remember back to you earliest swimming memory? Were you wearing floaties? Did you have a fun time with friends? Be specific and get into a lot of detail. If you can't remember a detail, make it up and make it interesting.

Name _____ Date _____

153. Imagine you have suddenly been transported into the body of the calorie-guzzling, gold medal-winning body of Michael Phelps. How do you cope with this newfound athletic machinery? Can you win more gold medals in the next Olympics? Do you even like swimming?

154. Write about your most memorable heavy rainstorm. Were you alone or with friends? Were you outside caught in it or were you in a car or house watching the rain splash down? Be specific and go into great detail about the rain itself and how it affected the world around you.

Name _____ Date _____

155. What would you do if all of your possessions were ruined in a
hurricane and flood? Elaborate about all that was lost and how you are going to have to
live your new life.

156. Write about the most fun you've ever had at a water park or on a water ride. If you
haven't been to one, make up the most elaborate water slide ever and detail your journey
through it.

Name _____ Date _____

157. Describe in extreme detail a shower or bath. Talk about your
process through it and make some connection between the cleansing and your life. For
example, you could be washing the feeling of working a 9 to 5 job away with the shower.
Feel free to make up some subtext for it.

158. You are in high school and throwing the best pool party ever! Go through the
planning of it all the way through the exciting water filled excitement.

Name _____ Date _____

159. Imagine you are a goldfish trapped in a little fish bowl. How do you get through the boredom of everyday life?

160. Write a scene with your favorite water animals having a conversation about their lives as if they were human.

Name _____ Date _____

161. Describe the experience when you've felt closest to nature. Try to remember a time in which you were truly affected by the natural world and it became a major part of who you are. If that's never happened, make it up.

162. Imagine that one day, all plant life and animals just started to talk to you. They talk to some other people too, so it's not like you're crazy. What do they tell you and what do you do about it?

Name _____ Date _____

163. You wake up one day as a frog on a lily pad. What do you do
and how do you get back to your human form? Is this a Disney fairy tale (light and fluffy)
or a Grimm's fairy tale (dark and ominous)?

164. Do you have a personal plan to preserve nature in your community? Even if you only
spend 5 minutes a day each week, what is it you could plan to do with that time? Do you
even want to preserve nature?

Name _____ Date _____

165. Talk about a big hike or nature trail walk that you've been on. If you never have, make it up. Who were you with, what did you bring, and why do you remember it so well?

166. If you had a choice of any natural landscape to live in on the planet and money was not a problem where would you live? What would your first year there be like?

Name _____ Date _____

167. What is your favorite season and why? What personal
memories have occurred during that season? Go into extreme detail on what you like about
that season and mention what it is you don't like about the other ones.

168. Your favorite natural area is about to be changed into a shopping mall. What do you
do to stop it and how do you get the community on your side?

Name _____ Date _____

169. In a horror-movie setting, nature fights back. You are stuck in the middle of a forest at night. How do you get out of this predicament and back into civilization?

170. For some reason, as if you were a Disney princess, animals of the forest begin to come out of nowhere to help you through your life. What do you do with this newfound power?

Name _____ Date _____

171. You can grow the garden of your choice without money or time as a hindrance. What do you grow and why? How do you keep out the rabbits?

172. Describe an experience in which you and ten friends all begin climbing an ancient and amazing looking tree.

©2012 Build Creative Writing Ideas

Name _____ Date _____

173. Talk about a time in which it really felt like you were using your animal instincts. This could be a time where you really felt your body and emotions took over. It could be positive or negative. Be very specific about how it felt and how you reacted afterward.

174. If you could be any animal, what would you be and why? Detail a typical day in the life of this new animal version of you.

Name _____ Date _____

175. What is your opinion on the mistreatment of animals in some slaughterhouses and chicken farms? Do you feel it is your personal responsibility to help these animals or do you feel as though the efficiency of the process is in the name of human progress? Be very specific and detailed.

176. If any mythical creature could be actually alive (unicorn, Sasquatch, ewok) which one would it be and why? Then, create a story of your discovery of this animal and how to peacefully bring it to the world's attention.

Name _____ Date _____

177. Who was/is your favorite childhood pet and why? Talk about
some of your experiences with this pet and why you'll always keep him or her in your
memory.

178. Who was/is your least favorite childhood pet and why? What are some of the things
that turned you off of this pet? Do you blame the pet? Are the breeders or owners at fault?

Name _____ Date _____

179. You have become a bird! How does the world look to you now
that you can fly through the air at great speed? What are the things you have to worry
about?

180. If you could have any animal as a pet (that you have not previously had in your life)
what would it be and why? Talk about some of your adventures with this pet and see how
he or she adjusts to your current lifestyle.

Name _____ Date _____

181. You have become a zookeeper! You take care of pretty much everything in the zoo from the penguins to the elephants. What is it like being on the other side of the cage (assuming that you aren't already a zookeeper)? Talk about one of your typical days.

182. In a bit straight out of *The Island of Dr. Moreau* you are creating new animals by adding different parts from different animals together. What kind of crazy combinations have you created? How are you dealing with the consequences of bringing something semi-unnatural into the world?

Name _____ Date _____

183. Imagine life as part of a culture that truly values animals and requires them directly for various parts of life (like the Native Americans and buffalos). How is your life different and what is a typical day like for you?

184. Talk about one technology that you feel as though you could never live without. Is it television? Would you die without text messaging or the game pong? Detail your obsession with this technology and write about a week in which it is taken away from you.

Name _____ Date _____

185. Imagine that television, movies, etc. were never invented. How would your family have spent the evening time when you were growing up? Do you feel as though this would have changed your family dynamic at all?

186. What if you created the next new important technology? What would it be and how would it change the world? Be creative here, don't just make up something that would be a two-day fad and then pass.

Name _____ Date _____

187. PC or Mac and why? This is a simple prompt, but so many
people are extremely passionate about this choice. Have fun with this one.

188. How would your life have been different if you'd grown up 20 years earlier? What
about 10 years earlier or 10 years later? What about 20 years later? How would technology
have affected your life differently? Would you be a different person today (other than age-
wise)?

Name _____ Date _____

189. Your sci-fi prompt of the hour! A technologically advanced alien race has come to Earth wanting to trade information. What new technological advances do we pick up from them and do we use them for good and evil? How does the diplomacy go with these aliens?

190. Do you feel as though technology has changed your relationships with other people? Do you consider your interpersonal connection better or worse with the innovations of texting, Twitter, Facebook, and the like? Be specific and cite several examples.

Name _____ Date _____

191. Talk about a time in your life where technology most helped you. It can be medically related, socially-related; really any time that technology affected you in a positive way.

192. Talk about a time in your life where technology most hurt you. This story can involve any time that technology in any form got in your way of something, slowed you down, or literally hurt you. Be very specific.

Name _____ Date _____

193. You have been transported back to the Middle Ages with a couple of types of technology. How do you survive and how do you get back to the present day?

194. Describe a week at a meditation camp in which technology is not allowed for an entire week. Is it peaceful to be "unplugged" or are you a frantic mess?

Name _____ Date _____

195. What is your favorite website and why? Talk about how much time you spend on it per week and the ways in which it fulfills you. What would happen if it was taken away from you?

196. You have been shrunk down to the size of a byte and you are bouncing around on the Internet! What does everything look and feel like? How do you get around and how are you going to get out of there?

Name _____ Date _____

197. Talk about the weirdest place you've ever gotten Internet. A Wi-Fi cafe in a foreign country? On your iPhone while you're in a restroom? Describe the situation and talk about what a person would have thought about that phenomenon only 20 years ago.

198. Several people have talked about being pioneers of the Internet. Create a humorous story in which a rag tag bunch of nerdy programmers create the Internet and then have their ideas stolen by someone else.

Name _____ Date _____

199. Do you feel as though the Internet has improved your connection with people or has it taken away from that connection? Use several examples and feel free to craft a story of online social awkwardness with it.

200. Talk about a time in which you had an Internet misunderstanding, whether it was through email, instant message, Facebook, Twitter, or anywhere else. If you do not have such a time, make one up. Feel free to elaborate and exaggerate.

Extra Page

Name _____ Date _____

ABOUT THE AUTHOR

Bryan Cohen is a writer, actor and director who grew up in Dresher, Pennsylvania just outside of Philadelphia. He graduated from the University of North Carolina at Chapel Hill with degrees in English and Dramatic Art along with a minor in Creative Writing. His books on writing prompts and writing motivation have sold over 10,000 copies and they include *1,000 Creative Writing Prompts: Ideas for Blogs, Scripts, Stories and More*, *1,000 Character Writing Prompts: Villains, Heroes and Hams for Scripts, Stories and More*, *500 Writing Prompts for Kids: First Grade through Fifth Grade*, *1,000 Character Writing Prompts: Villains, Heroes and Hams for Scripts, Stories and More* and *The Post-College Guide to Happiness*. Cohen continues to produce and perform plays and films in between his books and freelance writing work. He lives in Chicago.

Made in the USA
Middletown, DE
27 June 2023

33962158R00064